# A Poetry Book for Sad, Messy Teenagers

By Gracie Adams

ISBN: 9781081751579

Warning to readers:

Before you go ahead and read these poems, I beg of you that you read this first. This collection of poems was written during an extremely dark time for me. Please note that I am doing well now, so great in fact that my main emotion is happiness. If you are in a dark place as well, do not allow these poems to romanticize your feelings and thoughts. I know what it's like to be where you are, but take this collection of poems as a sign that someone who felt your pain got better and is now happy. That being said, look for the sequel: It Gets Better B*tch. Please enjoy, and if you need help please call the following numbers*:

Call 1-800-273-8255 for National Suicide Prevention Lifeline

Call 240-485-1001 for Anxiety and Depression Association of America (ADAA)

Call 800-826-3632 for Depression and Bipolar Support Alliance (DBSA)

Call 617-973-5801 for information on OCD and treatment referrals Text CONNECT to 741741 for help with self-harm




*All phone numbers are current as of date of first publication

Have you ever been so sad
To the point where it physically hurts

I'm losing myself more and more
Every
Single
Day

Sometimes all you can do is lie down
Begging your mind and body to fall asleep
Before you fall apart

And all of a sudden
Sad songs aren't sad anymore
Because you've seen sadder

I wish to lay in the street when it's raining
So that I can drown
In something that isn't my own thoughts

All the hope that's in my body is being drained out
My scars may be healing but I am most certainly not
We're all just suicidal kids
Preaching to all the other suicidal kids that killing yourself isn't an option
Just a bunch of fuck ups telling each other that it'll get better
But we all know the truth

We will never find a cure for our ill souls

For we're intoxicated with the sadness
And infatuated with the madness

Maybe we aren't afraid of dying,
But of our names being stolen
Instead of us,
Silence is what fills the room
Voices that aren't ours
For we never really know
How long each lifespan is
How many years we will be relevant
After our bodies turn to dust
Maybe it will be around for generations
Maybe it will disappear after hours
Maybe it will last until the space is filled
Perhaps it will live forever
It will live even after we fade
I mean that's why we become writers
Poets, musicians, actors, producers
To write our names on something
The books we create
The music that we make
All we've ever made
Ever done
It's a sliver of meaning
In a society prone to forget
We have hope
That they'll find the stories that we left
They'll stumble upon our half written pages
And notebooks covered with words
With our names on the bottom of the cover page
And just for one moment, one second,
We escaped death
Because someone wasted our name
On a perfectly good breath.

The world
Does not start
Being happy
When you stop
Being sad

you're going to break my heart anyways
there's no preventing it

Your soul
is where
I made myself
a home out of
broken bones

Express to me
that I am not forgettable
Not as forgettable
as the silence
in the air
is making me feel

One of my most
monumental trepidations
Is that I will die
Without finding one soul
That cherishes the fire
that lies behind my eyes

it's pointless
to make someone a priority
when you're at
the bottom of their list

We have rib cages
To keep our demons
From hurting anyone
Other than
Ourselves

I'm scared because at this point
I don't even know what the hell is wrong with me
They say to ignore your brain and follow your heart
But my brain thinks I'm worthless and my heart agrees

meds>therapy
change the chemicals in your brain
shrinks will only steal your money

Hello.

Hi.
 Guess what.
What?

*Fuck you.*

I'm in the backseat of my own car
Confined by the belt
And tortured by the stereo
Manipulated by the driver
And blindfolded from the keys
All I know is that
I'm in the backseat of my own fucking car

I love you
And I know you're busy
But can you give me
The decency
Of five fucking minutes

my chemical imbalance is giving me a headache

you don't get to choose how your words affect me.
understand this.
you shattered me.
and you've lost my trust.
when all of your new friends leave don't expect to find me.
cause i'll be gone too.

i tell my mom everything and she hates you

i just read our break up texts for inspiration
and even though i'm over it
my heart kind of stings

i can't trust myself
and i can't trust you not to leave again
because i can't read your mind
and i'm obviously not as good
as your other friends.

Anxiety turns non-existent problems
Into catastrophes
It interrupts the sleep that you need
To the point where you physically cannot keep your eyes open anymore
Problems that were once not relevant are blasted into your mind
It's like having the angel and devil on your shoulders
Except the angel is taking a life-long break
And the devil won't shut his god damned mouth
Silently whispering
All of the things that can go wrong today
Making sure that you know that you're worthless
Are the whispers in my ear little truths that I fail to see
I feel like an elephant is sitting on my chest

I've been fighting against my demons for so long
I tried to win
But they're screaming louder than ever
And fighting harder
I don't want to fight anymore
I give up
They win.

People aren't losing much
once they drop me
My existence
would merely be
a distant memory

I
Dont
Give
A
Fuckedy
Fuck
Anymore

Can you just understand
That I don't understand
Why I am the way I am
I don't understand
And I never will
And that is what I need you
To understand

I am intoxicatingly dangerous
But only to myself

Let us let Love give us his lie
Before we accept Death's truth
Let us believe that we have the audacity
To think that we are crucial to this universe
Before we realize that there's so many people
on this miserably sweet planet that matter
more

Let us stand up
Before we find out that we most certainly
Will fall down again

Let us look at the fogged sky
Oblivious to the fact that stars once roamed
the darkness

Let us live our extremely inadequate life
Before Death sweeps us away off of our feet

"Why aren't you talking"
Because I'll always be wrong right?
That's the point.
No matter what I do or what I say I'll never be the one that's right, I'll only ever be the one that is wrong.
Because I'm a kid and you're an adult
Because kids are too young to be right
And adults are too old to be wrong
And at some point
I have to be tired of fighting
So I fight myself instead
And every time they yell at me
Or call me names
Or act like I don't exist
I'm silent
Because I know that later that night
When no one's awake
I'll be crying alone
With your hurtful words in mind

branching out
doesn't mean
leaving your old friends behind
you bitch

You want a happy poem?
O k a y.


Roses are red
Violets are blue
My mind is fucked up
Happy poems are shit

how broken do i need to be
before you're happy

but you threw me away
without telling me why
or that you were
and that hurt too
that broke me in so many ways

how could you let me go to sleep
thinking that you hate me?
that is so fucking cruel.
but once again you're the fucking victim

What is normal for the shark
Is agony for the fish

People scare me
They have the power to change your life in a matter of moments
That's why I don't trust easily
Because being in that state of vulnerability
Is so god damned scary
To allow someone to hold your heart in their hands
People are much scarier than demons
At least demons make it clear that they are going to hurt you
People try to hide it
That's why I dance with my demons
And ignore my angels

i can't wait for people on instagram and twitter
to read this and hate me

i'm the most insensitive sensitive asshole i know

No one knows
When we stop ticking
We aren't broken clocks

you inhale and exhale repugnance
creeping suicidal tendencies
you don't care anymore about anything
the only thing keeping you awake
are the nightmares
the salty water
the depth of reality
you feel that even death
is more appealing
than this self-sadism

the anger that i have
for certain human beings
is un-fucking real

holy SHIT you're annoying

my heart is slowly decaying
my mind is slowly fading
you broke me in more ways than one

the sane
and the psycho
shared the same madness

HA! fuck you

All I do is try to make people happy
Because I know all too well
What it's like to be at the bottom of an abyss
I don't want anyone to feel that way
I began to care more for others feelings
Than my own
Somewhat because I knew that no one really cared anyways
I want to scream my miseries to people
I want to slide down a wall
Curl up in a ball
And cry
And never stop crying
Until the pain is gone
But all I can do is stare at the ceiling
And listen to others
And try to help others
I've never felt so alone yet so needed
But needed for the wrong reasons
People don't need me to become happy
People need me as a distraction
And distractions are always replaceable
…
It's so much simpler
To fake a smile
Rather than to explain to others how you really feel
I don't think that everyone knows
What it is like
To be tortured by your own mind
The thoughts that I think are not safe
Are not positive
Are not made by me
It is because of that
That I listen to other people's thoughts
And how they hate themselves
Cause maybe if I replace my problems
With others
Mine will go away

I don't know
Sometimes
I think I'm over all of this
But I know
I know that things have just gotten worse
Because everything is shoved down
In the garbage can of my mind

i haven't stopped crying
my heart's been hurting
i need a distraction in my brain
i don't want to be here
my demon's whispering the sins that
he swore he'd never speak of again
the evil devours him
it makes him the demon that he ought to always
be
he screeches so i know
he exists
and he will never leave me alone

You have two options in life:
1) You can spend seconds, minutes, hours, days, weeks, months, even years trying to figure out what went wrong; or
2) You can move the fuck on

I didn't realize
until the end
that it was
all a lie

But it was
a believable one
for a time

They told me to pick my poison
So I chose you
And you haven't failed
To meet their
expectations

I blur my sadness for the most part
That's why everyone thinks I'm happy

I push people away
Not because I don't like them
But because they won't be happy around me
And I don't want to be the cause of someone's sadness

I need a break from myself
Because even though I don't like making people sad
I find that I can't stop myself from being the reason for my own sadness

i'm sorry that i left you when you probably
needed me the most
after all
we were both pretty fucked up

You were always my favorite thing in the world
Because I was light
And attracted to you, the darkness
Little did I know
How much darkness covered the light
And suddenly I was the dark
And you were the light
That's when you left
When you realized that you could live
Rather than just exist

The most beautiful form of wrecking myself
Was loving you

death and joy

are fused in a tempestuous way
where soul and heart are best friends
and dive in the unpredictable

i'll leave your ass on read until the day i die

i hate the sound
of the words
i love you
when they come out of
your mouth

i warn other girls about you
you fucking disgusting pervert
i said no
i said no
i said no
and you didn't fucking listen

Most of my scars
were created
in his name

Why do I expect
to find a peaceful escape
When I am
in the middle
of a chaotic storm

One day
My demons will die
Leaving me alone in this world
Because while they hurt me
They were the only ones there
When I needed you the most

I knew it was over
When the psychopath
Was deemed normal after sitting next to me

I am the light that you will never deserve
And you are the darkness that I will forever
be attracted to

I hate night
Cause that's when I cry
Which is such a sight
I sometimes just want to die
I hate to rhyme
I'm trying to be sad
Now is not the time
Okay now you're making me mad

Alright fuck you

I am so sick and tired
Of repeating history
It's exhausting
To go through the same shit with the same
people over and over again

i didn't mean it when i said i love you
it was never true
it was a mistake
you'll find someone
but you and i were never meant to be
                    -To myself from myself

We are all ripped to shreds
But together we make a beautiful masterpiece

Where is the light they told me was at the end of the tunnel?
At this point
I honestly just don't care
Regardless of if there is or isn't a light
I just want to get out of this toxic tunnel

It's a vicious cycle
To say hello and goodbye to your demons
over and over and over again

Just because I don't
Fit into your category
Doesn't mean that
I don't understand

When you left you took a part of me with you
A chapter is missing from the story of my soul
A blank space in the middle of my mind
And a boundless emptiness is in my heart

You promised to fix my broken heart
But you damaged it more
Until there was nothing left
But the strands of a ravaged soul
Keeping a body alive

When I die
My death certificate
Will be woefully incorrect
Because we all know
That I died
Long before
My time

I was arrested by society
And put in a cell surrounded by reality

There is not nearly enough
Water in the ocean
To clean away
The stains on my heart
That you made

i didn't mean to say i love you back
but i did under the constraints of your
pathetic way
i'm sorry
i shouldn't have said it when i didn't mean it
you're crying now
because you found out i actually fucking hate
you

Woah. I HATE myself 😊

My heart is still mourning the loss of you
But my brain can't help but think
That your death
Was the absolute best thing for me

I've always wondered how love works
It wasn't until you broke my heart
That I realized it doesn't

God didn't mean to make me
i'm just the leftovers from the perfect batch
that he created

My visible scars
Are nothing
Compared to the ones
That lay beyond my skin

I'm so exhausted

I don't want to know
What the square root of 78,268,139 is
What I want is to learn
How to be happy
But to my dismay
They don't teach that to you in school

I can't keep doing
What I have been doing
For the last couple of years

I was drowning
And you were watching from the side
Yelling at me to just swim
But you can't swim when you don't know how
And you don't have anybody to guide you

Why do I feel so lost
When all I am
Is stuck inside
The abyss
Of my own mind

I am not beautiful

Once you die
Society moves on without you

It could've been prevented.
If only . . .

If only you weren't stubborn.
If only you listened.
If only you went to the doctor.
If only you weren't sick.
If only you didn't always deny the fact that you weren't feeling well.
If only you made the call.
If only you went to the hospital weeks before.

If only it wasn't too late.
If only it was a dream.
If only it didn't happen to you.

If only I could have prevented it.
If only I had forced you to see someone.
If only I could build a time machine.
If only I asked you if you were okay more often.
If only I could've been around more.
If only I dragged you to the doctor.
If only I could go back.
If only I said goodbye in time.

But it's too late . . .
You're gone.

You and your sister have the same face.
It hurts every time I see her, cause I also see you.
I miss you.
She misses you. She's not the same since you left.
She sees the light in life, but it's harder when you're not there to guide her.
She's different, she's changed.

I've changed.
I'm not the same.

It's been what, four years?
Four years without you.
Four years ago cancer took you away.
You fought beautifully.
But it wasn't enough to keep you here.
It wasn't enough to save the kindest soul that God has ever created.

If only you were here...
If only cancer didn't exist.
If only I could go on with life.
If only there wasn't a gaping hole in my heart where you should be.

If only—

You never
had the power
to hurt me
I was broken long before
you entered my life

While it is true that I was not the one that made you feel the need to run at night

I most certainly wasn't the one that made you feel safe enough to walk in the dark

The devil asked me
Why I chose to go to hell
For I could've gone to heaven
However I didn't know it as well
In heaven I'd need a map
And the angels they'd only yell
Yes, I am good, but I'm also fucked up
The lightness never rang a bell
The darkness however
Oh how the darkness cast a spell
On my broken little heart
The demons are so swell
I understand hell you see Mr.Devil
Heaven would never be able to compel
Nor could I trick it
Into thinking that I fit
When I know the deep and powerful darkness
All too well

He killed me
My soul I mean
It was always my soul that he was after

We can talk about my sins
Now that I've been punished

I abandoned myself
Into your eyes
Deceitful eyes where nothing
But the truth
Could lie

When someone hurts you
Pain and apologies
Are delivered in unison

I will be punished by my sins
Not because of them

I have to resist the urge to throw daggers
Into the fuckers I hate

I love
Absolutely love
The simplicity
Of those who simply
Don't give a fuck

When I'm older
And not just a pile of damaged goods
If I ever
Find myself living an insufficient life
I sure do hope
That I have the guts
To go out and change it

Am I broken now?
Yes
We all are
But I have sworn to myself
That I will find the glue
And put myself back together
No matter how long it takes
I will be happy
I can promise myself that much
I will not always be a depressed little shit
One day
The tape will be found
The pieces will merge back together
I will be untroubled
But I'll be damned
If I'm on my death bed
Looking back at an unsatisfactory life
Cause It Gets Better B*tch

Printed in Great Britain
by Amazon